What the Spirits are Saying

What the Spirits are Saying

Shari Flusche

authorHOUSE®

AuthorHouse™
1663 Liberty Drive
Bloomington, IN 47403
www.authorhouse.com
Phone: 1-800-839-8640

Published by AuthorHouse   08/16/2012

ISBN: 978-1-4772-6191-0 (sc)
ISBN: 978-1-4772-6192-7 (e)

Library of Congress Control Number: 2012915035

REPRODUCED BY PERMISSION OF THE COPYRIGHT OWNERS:

1. *Quotations taken from The Holy Bible, New International Version, Copyright 1973, 1978, 1984 by International Bible Study. Zondervan NIV Study Bible (Fully Revised) Copyright 1985, 1995, 2002 by Zondervan. All rights reserved. Published by Zondervan; Grand Rapids, MI 49530. www.zondervan.com.*

2. *Quotations are taken from "Praying Effectively for the Lost". 2003, by Lee E. Thomas; P.O. Box 1058, Westlake, LA 70669. Tel. 337 433-2663. www.pelministries.org. All rights reserved.*

3.   Quotations are taken from "The Pieta Prayer Book". 2004, by MLOR Corporation; 1186 Burlington Drive, Hickory Comers, MI 49060-9330. Tel. 269 731-4490. www.mlor.com. Printed in U.S.A. All rights reserved.

4.   Quotations are taken from "There is More to the Secret". 2007, by Ed Gungor. Published in Nashville, TN by Thomas Nelson, Inc. All rights reserved.

5.   Quotations are taken from "How to Hear God's Voice, by Mark Virkler and Patti Virkler, ISBN 10-076842318X. 2006. Published by Destiny Image Publishers: P. O. Box 310; Shippensburg, PA 17257-0310. www.destinyimage.com. All rights reserved.

6.   Quotations are taken from "Angels in our Lives" by Marie Chapian ISBN Nos. 0768423708, 9780768423709. 2006. Published by Destiny Image Publishers;   P. O. Box 310; Shippensburg, PA 17257-0310. wwwdestinyimage.com. All rights reserved.

7.   Quotations are taken from "90 Minutes in Heaven" by Don Piper w/Cecil Murphy. 2005. Publisher: Baker Book House. www.bakerpublishinggroup.com.

Contents

DECLARATION

The decree of the Congregation for the Propagation of the Faith, A.A.S.58, 1186 (approved by Pope Paul VI on October 14, 1966) states that the NILHIL OBSTAT and IMPRIMATUR are no longer required on publication that deal with private revelations, provided they contain nothing contrary to faith and morals.

We wish to manifest our conditional submission to the final and official judgment of the Magisterial of the Church for any of the enclosed or private revelations.

WHAT THE SPIRITS ARE SAYING

The Day of the Lord

"And afterward, I will pour out my Spirit on all people. Your sons and daughters will prophesy, your old men will dream dreams, your young men will see visions. Even on my servants, both men and women, I will pour out my Spirit in those days. I will show wonders in the heavens and on earth, blood and fire and billows of smoke. The sun will be turned to darkness and the moon to blood before the coming of the great dreadful day of the Lord. And everyone who calls on the name of the Lord will be saved." (Joel 2:28-32.)

God bless this book. God bless all the words in this book.

Heavenly Father,
I humbly ask you to give your very best blessing to all who read this book. Lord, open their hearts and minds to your Word so they may become spiritually healed and learn the truth. Lord, give them wisdom, knowledge and understanding of your Word, so that it will become effective in their lives.

Please send down your Holy Spirit and guardian angels to guide all of their thoughts, words and actions so that they may be of yours and pleasing to you. I plead the power of the Blood of Christ for their salvation and your greater glory. Amen.

Introduction

"For God's gift and His call are irrevocable." (Romans 11:29)

The reason I am writing this book is to help save souls, to defeat the devil. I am not writing this for personal gain. It's not about me. I would much rather keep to myself.

This is about what God wants us to know about what the devil is doing to us and how we can overcome, be set free, and be saved despite all the adversity the devil throws our way.

My sister-in-law passed away on November 14, 2007. She was only 46 years old, a beautiful person, taken by cancer. If it were not for her, this book would not have been written. You see, I have been praying certain prayers for the salvation of souls. When I prayed these prayers for her, she answered me. She said, "You are being selfish by not telling others what you know."

After several months of doubt, I finally realized that this is God's Will for my life. My Mom and I were at a Christian bookstore when it came to me that these prayers need to be said for every soul, living and dead.

This book is written through the inspiration of God. I had been trying to get my thoughts together and organized to no avail. Then, on February 6, 2008, Ash Wednesday, God woke me up at 3 a.m. and spoke to me, "If you are going to write this book, now is the time."

I had my usual excuses. I don't know how to write a book, I don't know where to begin; plus, the doubts the devil put on my mind—there are already books written on praying for the salvation of souls. Also, I've only been born-again for 5 years and I don't know God's Word well enough to write a book this important, and I will look like an ignorant fool if I write this book.

Every doubt I had, God had an answer for. When I thought I needed more information on spirits, God led me to the book, "Angels in Our Lives", by Marie Chapian. Wow! She teaches you how to experience and live in the spiritual world, and how to never limit what God can do. Marie Chapian is a minister, Bible teacher, and author of more than 30 books. She has been studying God's Word for most of her life.

So now I'm thinking, "Why me, Lord?" I'm too stupid. I don't know God's Word well enough to write a book this important. So, I went to the book store hoping to find more knowledge on the subject. I was thrilled when I found "Mother Teresa, Come be my Light". The answer I got from this book was not at all what I was expecting. I thought I would learn to be strong in doing God's Will through inspiration for Mother Teresa's life. It was the opposite. Mother Teresa experienced great suffering, doubt, loneliness, feelings of lack of self-worth and confidence in herself. She did not understand why God called her because she felt she was the most unworthy and sinful one so full of weakness, of misery and sin.

I could relate to all her feelings of inadequacy. Mother Teresa also searched for proof that this call was indeed God's Will and not some delusion, just as I was searching.

God was telling me that he chooses the weak because we totally surrender to His Will. We don't try to use our own words or do it our own way. **It is all His.**

Shortly after reading this book, I was watching Joyce Meyer on TV and she said, "God chooses the lowly. When Dave and I first started this ministry, we didn't know what we were doing. Fear is Satan's tool that keeps you from being the person God wants you to be." Marie Chapian says in her book, "Angels in our Lives", 'Don't ever be surprised at things God does or the people God chooses.' God was again reinforcing that I could do this. This is the call He has for my life. "But He said to me, 'My grace is sufficient for you, for my power is made perfect in weakness.' Therefore, I will boast all the more gladly about my weaknesses, so that Christ's power may rest on me. That is why, for Christ's sake I delight in weaknesses, in insults, in hardships, in persecutions, in difficulties. For when I am weak, them I am strong." (2Corinthians 12:9-10)

"Choosing the Lord's mind, thoughts and actions over my own is elementary—the Bible says, **'The fear of the Lord is the beginning of knowledge**.' The fear of the Lord is the state of mind where our attitudes, will, feelings, deeds, and goals are exchanged for God's. The angels partner with me as I choose the Lord's mind, thought, and actions over my own." (Angels in Our Lives, Pg. 77)

When I had the doubt that people will think I am crazy, God showed me that I'm not the only one experiencing visions and spiritual phenomenon. In an interview, Josh Turner told about his blessed life. He stated that when he was 9 years old, he had a vision of Jesus. He asked the Lord, "Why did you let me see this?" The Lord told him, "Josh, I'm going to take you a long way from Hannah, South Carolina and I want you to always know that I exist, no matter what happens, no matter who you get around, no matter what kind of experiences you have in your life. I want you to think back in your life and know that I'm real." Josh also had a vision of a dark train and people standing around trying to decide whether to get on or not. He knew the train presented temptations, and it led to his writing, "Long Black Train", his debut hit single about choices we make and resisting temptation.

Through all my doubts, the spirits kept telling me, "We will help you! Just sit down and write your story from the beginning to end as it happened."

I thought of my uncle who had just written a new song, who, when asked how he did it, said, "It was just like Alan Jackson said on TV, I just held the pencil.

So I finally gave in to God's Will and said, "Okay, but all I'm going to do is hold the pencil." What follows is what God wants the world to know.

Chapter One

My Own Personal Sanctification and Conviction from God

"My prayer is not that you take them out of the world but that you protect them from the evil one. They are not of the world, even as I am not of it. Sanctify them by the Truth, your word is Truth." (John 17:15-17) (Jesus praying for his disciples.)

Who am I to write a book of this caliber, one that God said the whole world needs to read, if they know what is good for them. I am just an A-B student who was fairly good in English class, at best. I am from a small town of 1500 population, who almost completed a Secretarial Science degree at a local college, but I dropped out after I cut my boyfriend's hair for the first time. It was so fun! I enrolled in Cosmetology school a.s.a.p.

To make a long story short, I worked as a hair stylist for 13 years. I started in 1990 and my parents helped me get my own shop in 1991. That same year I got married. In 1994, we built a house and had our first child. We now have 3 beautiful children, ages 13, 15 and 17. I thought it was the perfect life and I guess it was pretty good because that is when the devil showed up to ruin it all. I started to dread going to work. I was burnt out after 10 years of doing hair, but worked three more years after that which were the hardest years of my life so far. I knew in my heart this wasn't right because God didn't put us on earth to be miserable. He wants us to be happy. "I know that there is nothing better for men than to be happy and do good while they live." (Ecclesiastes 3:12)

Everything at work started to get on my nerves like never before, especially the gossip. I started hating myself and who I was becoming. (In hindsight I realize this feeling was from God sanctifying and convicting me.) Even though my heart knew everything was going wrong, my mind and other people kept telling me not to quit. "The devil can rule your mind, but God is in your heart, so listen to your heart." (Joyce Meyers)

I continued to listen to my mind and everyone else. I always thought this was what I was going to do for the rest of my life. Sometimes things have to change for us to grow spiritually to become the person that God wants us to be. Change is always for the better if we are following God's Will for our life.

I kept asking God for a sign if I should quit doing hair or not, and He kept giving them, but I kept listening to my mind which kept saying, "What will I do if I quit doing hair? I am not qualified to do anything else."

Then one day at work I finally got the sign I needed to make my decision to quit. The business sign fell off of the building and landed on the hood of a customer's new car. That was it. That was finally the "sign" I needed to quit.

After I quit, I went to work at Wal-Mart on the night shift because I was completely burnt out with dealing with the public. I thought I was going through a mid-life crisis. Now I can see God was sanctifying and convicting me to surrender my life to Him. He separated me from everything and everyone in my life, except my immediate family.

In her book, "Angels in Our Lives", pg. 151, Marie Chapian described it as her 'desert experience'. She said, "The Lord pulled me out of the busy life I had been leading and tucked me away alone with Him in a desert of my own. This went on for 3-1/2 years. Everyday, all day! I poured myself out before Him, and he poured Himself out for me."

God was calling me to pray, and boy did I ever! Previously, in my life, my prayers consisted of the 'Our Father' and the Guardian Angel' prayer at night before falling asleep. Now, my prayers turned into crying, screaming, and shouting to God, "Why is this happening? What's going on? What am I doing at a night job away from my family?" I knew there had to be a bigger purpose for my life than this. I could only find comfort in God's Word.

"By the power of God, who has saved us and called us to a holy life . . . not because of anything we have done, but because of His own purpose and grace." (2Timothy 1:8-9)

"In Him we were chosen, having been predestined according to the plan of Him who works out everything in conformity with the purpose of His Will." (Ephesians 1:11)

"There are different kinds of gifts, but the same Spirit, There are different kinds of service, but the same Lord. There are different kinds of working, but the same God works all of them in all men. Now to each one the manifestation of the Spirit is given for the common good. To one there is given through the Spirit the message of wisdom, to another the message of knowledge by means of the same Spirit to another faith by the same Spirit, to another gifts of healing by the one Spirit, to another miraculous powers, to another prophecy, to another distinguishing between spirits, to another speaking in different kinds of tongues, and to still another the interpretation of tongues. All these are the work of the same Spirit, and **He gives them to each, just as He determines**." (1Cor. 12:4-11)

"I raised you up for this very purpose, that I might display my power in you and that my Name might be proclaimed in all the earth." (Romans 9:17)

"And we know that in all things God works for the good of those who love him, who have been called according to his purpose." (Romans 8:28)

Chapter Two

The First Prayer

"If any of you lacks wisdom, he should ask God, who gives generously to all without finding fault, and it will be given to him. But when he asks, he must believe and not doubt, because he who doubts is like a wave of the sea, tossed by the wind." (James 1:5-6)

"Be joyful always, pray continually, give thanks in all circumstances, for this is God's Will for you in Christ Jesus." (1 Thessalonians 5:16-18)

The night job was too hard on my family life. So, after a year I took a part-time bookkeeping job working for my Mom's former boss. Several weeks into the job I started to really question what I had gotten myself into. Why did God have me doing a job I didn't like? I had to deal with legal papers I didn't understand. I was supposed to balance his checkbook and I can't even balance my own.

I was in charge of opening the mail and one day a yellow book entitled, "Praying Effectively for the Lost" caught my eye.

This book literally saved my life. It taught me how to pray for lost souls blinded by the devil. I learned from this book not to take anything personal. When someone does something evil, it is not them, it is the devil working through them.

Along with my Mom, I used the yellow book as a reference to write the following prayer "**Open Heart and Mind Prayer**" to save souls:

"Heavenly Father, we humbly ask you to give your very best blessing to (__Names__). Please sanctify and convict them to believe in Jesus Christ as their Lord and Savior. Open their hearts and minds to your Word so they can become spiritually healed and learn the Truth. We pray for their understanding of your Word and that it will become effective in their lives. Please send down your Holy Spirit and guardian angels to guide all their thoughts, actions and words so that they might be of yours and pleasing to you. Guide them to treat each other with kindness (or whatever special need they have—be specific), according to your Will. We plead the power of the Blood of Christ for their salvation and your greater glory. Amen."

In his book, Lee E. Thomas explains and gives personal testimonies that praying with more than one person is more effective. "Again, I tell you that if two of you on earth agree about anything you ask for, it will be done for you by my Father in Heaven, for where two or three come together in my name, there am I with them." (Matthew 18:19-20)

So my Mom and I met each day to pray this prayer together for salvation of everyone we knew and everyone God revealed to us that needed it.

The part-time bookkeeping job was not enough to pay the bills, so I applied for a job at a local factory as an assembler. I liked the work, but again, in my heart I knew that this was not what I would he doing until my retirement.

I knew that God had called me to pray after reading "Praying Effectively for the Lost". In the book, Lee E. Thomas states that "God has placed praying for others the number one priority in our lives. Hear the cry of God's heart, 'I urge then, first of all, that requests, prayers, intercession and thanksgiving be made for all men. This pleases God our Savior who wants all men to be saved and to come to the knowledge of the Truth.' (1 Timothy 2:1-4). Since God desires for all men to be saved and since no one can be saved without prayer, is it any wonder that prayer tops the list of things God would have us do?"

Mom and I continued praying together every day for everyone we knew. One day I was feeling down because our prayers didn't seem to be working as quickly as we wanted them to, and God kept revealing more and more people to us that needed prayer. It was just like Lee E. Thomas said in 'Praying Effectively for the Lost', "One of Satan's favorite tactics is to make the situation look so impossible that we get discouraged and quit praying. The reason he does this is because he has absolutely no defense against prayer. The old saying is true that Satan trembles when he sees the weakest saint upon his knees. When you pray, Satan is being defeated even though you see no change in the circumstances." He also says, "Another crucial factor which can be so subtle as to make literally years of praying totally ineffective is our motive! Our primary motive in praying for the lost must be for God's glory (See John 15:8), but many times our motives are poisoned with pride and selfishness."

So I thought my motive wasn't pure because I was praying for my loved ones to be saved, and I could not see a change.

We must pray for God's greater glory, not to benefit ourselves, but Him alone.

Rev. Lee E. Thomas says in 'Praying Effectively for the Lost', pg. 19, "Sharing the gospel with those for whom no one has prayed is like encouraging a blind man to view a beautiful sunset with you. It is a hopeless case, for he is blind. He cannot see! And unless the Holy Spirit removes the demonic blinders and opens his mind and heart to the gospel, he cannot be saved because the things of God are 'foolishness to him'." (1Cor. 1:25). The Greek word for foolishness is 'moria' from which moron is derived. So, a lost person sees the gospel as moronic and stupid, but it is the 'strong man' (Satan) in his life that causes this negative attitude toward the gospel. The word of God is to Satan as kryptonite is to Superman. It makes him weak and defenseless. It also decimates his kingdom by freeing his captives for 'Ye shall know the truth and the truth shall set you free.' (John 8:32); but notice, it is not the truth that sets you free, but rather the truth you know. So Satan does everything he can to keep people from knowing the truth."

Since I became born-again, I couldn't get enough of God's Word. "The heart of the discerning acquires knowledge; the ears of the wise seek it out." (Proverbs 18:15)

"Then you will call upon me and come and pray to me, and I will listen to you. You will seek me and find me when you seek me with all of your heart. I will be found by you", declares the Lord. (Jeremiah 29:12-14). Yet, I was surrounded by people in my life who didn't seem to desire the same thing I did, except for my Mom who was the only one I could talk openly to about my 'new life in Christ'.

"Therefore if anyone is in Christ, he is a new creation, the old has gone; the new has come! (2Cor. 5:17)

But, it's what Jesus says to do, "And when you pray, do not be like the hypocrites, for they love to pray to be seen by men. But when you pray, go into your room, close the door and pray to your Father, who is unseen. Then your Father, who sees what is done in secret, will reward you." (Matthew 6:5-6)

My new life in Christ was a very lonely one. I cried and pleaded with God every day to show me His Will for my life because I felt so alone—so lost! God is supposed to be the most important thing in our life—we don't need anything, but Him.

"I consider that our present sufferings are not worth comparing with the glory that will be revealed in us." (Romans 8:18)

"Enter through the narrow gate. For wide is the gate and broad is the road that leads to destruction, and many enter through it. But small is the gate and narrow the road that leads to life and only a few find it." (Matthew 7:13-14)

As hard as it was not to do what everyone else was doing, doing what is right brings us closer to God. "Your worst day with God is better than your best day without Him. Favor with people doesn't last but favor with God is eternal. One nod from God is worth more than an arena full of applause." (Joyce Meyer)

"As for you, you were dead in your transgressions and sins, in which you used to live when you followed the ways of the world and the ruler of the kingdom of the air, (Satan) the spirit who is now at work in those who are disobedient. All of us also lived among them at one time, gratifying in the cravings of our sinful nature and following its desires and thoughts. Like the rest, we were by nature objects of wrath. But because of His great love for us, God, Who is rich in mercy, made us alive in Christ even when we were dead in transgressions—**it is by grace you have been saved**." (Ephesians 2:1-5)

Chapter Three

The Second Prayer

"We have different gifts, according to the grace given us. If a man's gift is prophesying, let him use it in proportion to his faith. If it is serving, let him serve, if it is encouraging, let him encourage, if it is contributing to the needs of others, let him give generously, if it is showing mercy, let him do it cheerfully." (Romans 12:6-8)

I continued to pray everyday even though my loneliness was unbearable. The only thing that kept me going was my children. I thank God for them every day.

"In some way, the Spirit helps us in our weakness. We do not know what we ought to pray for, but the Spirit himself intercedes for us with groans that words cannot express.

And he who searches our hearts knows the mind of the Spirit, because the Spirit intercedes for the saints in accordance with God's Will." (Romans 8:26-27)

I asked God why I had to work at this factory when He has called me to pray. That night I had a vision. Something woke me at 3 a.m. in the morning, yet my eyes were still closed. I saw a large hand with a long white sleeve trimmed in gold. There was a brilliant white light that shone from behind the hand and I knew that this was God's hand because the Bible says that He is so bright; ". . . Out of the brightness of His presence." (2Samuel 22:13). "His face was like the sun shining in all its brilliance." (Revelations 1:16). Then, I saw hundreds of smaller hands reaching up to God's hand, touching it and grabbing it. It was so beautiful, so intriguing, I wanted to see more, but it faded away. I opened my eyes and sat up in bed wondering what it meant. It came to me that I would help many people come to God, through prayer, working at that job.

Mom and I started praying together for 2 hours every day. Then, more on our own for everyone God revealed to us that needed prayer. I prayed going to work and coming home. I said Our Father's for the salvation of souls while doing housework. If I didn't know what to pray I would just say, "Jesus, Mary, I love you, save souls." (The Pieta Prayer Book). All I wanted to do was pray. I was addicted to it. "Find what makes you feel good, what resonates with your heart, and you will find yourself right in the center of God's Will." (Ed Gungor, There is More to the Secret, Pg. 108)

If my mind wasn't on God, then the devil would try to tempt me with sinful thoughts. Joyce Meyer said, "If you dwell on a negative thought long enough, it will keep you from God's best." So I had to "Pray without ceasing" (1Thes. 5-17), because the devil really hates prayer and tried to distract me any way he could.

God kept giving us more and more people to pray for. "We have to prove ourselves with little before God gives us a lot." (Matthew 25:21)

I would receive magazines in the mail with lists of people. Mom and I realized that we needed help to pray for all these people. Lee E. Thomas stated in his book that with three or more people praying together, prayers are answered right away. So Mom decided to join a local prayer group. When they never called her back, we knew this was not the solution. God had a better idea; one that we could not have thought of in our wildest imagination. Remember, never limit God!

One day at work, not long after I had the vision, I gave a Billy Graham pamphlet, entitled 'Don't be Left Behind' to a co-worker. He then gave me a little blue prayer book, entitled, 'The Pieta Prayer Book'. I couldn't wait to read all the prayers in the book. I read a couple on the way home that brought me to tears. I gave the book to my Mom right away and said, "Your have to read these prayers. They are so powerful!"

In the Pieta Prayer Book we discovered the "**Three Very Beautiful Prayers**". They are prayers to be said for someone who is dying or has died, asking God to forgive him of his sins so that he will have eternal life in heaven. The following prayers are quoted directly from The Pieta Prayer Book, pg.29:

"It is related that there once was a Pope in Rome who was surrounded by many sins. The Lord God struck him with a fatal illness. When he saw that he was dying, he summoned Cardinals, Bishops and learned persons and said to them: 'My dear friends! What comfort can you give me now that I must die, and when I deserve eternal damnation for my sins?' No one answered him. One of them, a pious curate named John, said, 'Father, why do you doubt the Mercy of God?' The Pope replied, 'What comfort can you give me now that I must die and fear that I'll be damned for my sins?' John replied, 'I'll read three prayers over you; I hope, you'll be comforted and that you'll obtain mercy from God!' The Pope was unable to say more. The curate and all those present knelt and said the following prayers:

1. **Lord Jesus Christ! Thou Son of God and Son of the Virgin Mary, God and Man! Thou Who in fear sweated blood for us on the Mount of Olives in order to bring peace and to offer Thy Most Holy Death to God, Thy Heavenly Father, for the salvation of this dying person ____(Name)_____. If it be, however, that by his sins he merits eternal damnation, then may it be deflected from him. This, O Eternal Father, through Our Lord Jesus Christ, Thy Dear Son, Who lives and reigns in union with Thee and the Holy Spirit, now and forever. Amen.**

2. **Lord Jesus Christ! Thou Who meekly died on the trunk of the Cross for us, submitting Thy Will completely to Thy Heavenly Father in order to bring peace and to offer Thy most Holy Death to Thy Heavenly Father in**

order to free this person ____(Name)_____ and to hide from him what he has earned with his sins, grant this O Eternal Father through Our Lord Jesus, Thy Son, Who lives and reigns with Thee in union with the Holy Spirit now and forever. Amen.

3. Lord Jesus Christ! Thou Who remained silent to speak through the mouths of the Prophets: I have drawn Thee to me through Eternal Love, which Love drew Thee from heaven into the body of the Virgin, which love drew Thee from the body of the Virgin into the valley of this needful world, which Love kept thee thirty-three years in this world. As a sign of great love, Thou hast given Thy Holy Body as true food and Thy Holy Blood as true drink. As a sign of great Love, Thou hast consented to be a prisoner and to be led from one judge to another. As a sign of great Love, Thou hast consented to be condemned to death, and to appear to Thy Holy Mother and all the holy apostles. As a sign of great Love Thou hast ascended under Thy own strength and power, and sits at the right hand of God, Thy Heavenly Father. Thou hast sent Thy Holy Spirit into the hearts of Thy Apostles and the hearts of all who hope and believe in Thee. Through Thy sign of Eternal Love, open heaven today and take this dying person ___(Name)___, and all his forgiven sins into the realm of Thy Heavenly Father, that he may reign with Thee now and forever. Amen.

Meanwhile the Pope dies. The curate persevered to the third hour. Then the Pope appeared to him in body and comforted him, his countenance as brilliant as the sun, his clothes as white as snow, and he said, 'My dear brother! Whereas I was supposed to be a child of damnation, I've become a child of happiness. As you recited the first prayer many of my sins fell from me as rain from heaven, and you recited the second prayer, I was purified as a goldsmith purifies gold in a hot fire; I was still further purified as you recited the third prayer. **Then I saw heaven open and the Lord Jesus standing at the right hand of God the Father, who said to me, "Come, all thy sins are forgiven thee, you'll be and remain in the realm of My Father forever. Amen!"**

With these words my soul separated from my body and the angels of God led it to eternal joy.' As the curate heard this he said, 'O Holy Father! I can't tell these things to anyone for they won't believe me.' Then the Pope said, 'Truly, I tell thee, the Angel of God stands with me and has written the prayers in letters of gold for the console of all sinners.'

Then the Pope said that these prayers, if they are recited in the presence of a great sinner who is about to die, will aid them with many graces and even assist them in their suffering in purgatory so that they will be freed from any punishments that are due to their sins.

He also said that the person who hears them read should himself trust that the Lord preserves him from an unhappy death. The story tells us that he even had them taken into St. Peter's Basilica and placed on the altar as a sign of his great esteem for them. He especially desired that anyone who recited these prayers would have the hour of his death revealed to him in order to make a good preparation and avoid purgatory."

Mom read the prayers in The Pieta Prayer Book from cover to cover. When she got to the three prayers, she did not know who was dying at the time, so she inserted the words, "For the next person who dies from Muenster". (For privacy sake, the name of this person has been changed.) About a week later, a man named Henry was killed in a severe auto accident. The following day, Mom was reading The Pieta Prayer Book and when she came to the "Three Very Beautiful Prayers", thought to herself, 'I wonder if this prayer worked for Henry?' At that moment, Henry spoke to her, "So you are the one who did this for me. They were not allowed to tell me who it was. Now, I owe you a favor, "What can I do for you?" She told him she wanted all her family to go to heaven when they die. "Could he help direct them in the right paths?" He said, "Yes!"

Henry proved to us that **these prayers also work if they are said for the living**. This prayer was God's answer to our request for help in saving souls! He has sent us the spirits to help us guide souls to Christ. The souls that we saved would return to us and ask us to say prayers for their relatives. We learned that when we say the "Open Heart and Mind Prayer" for someone, the spirits can help guide that person to make the right choices in life and come to Christ. It's the same principle as the Holy Spirit guiding us through our conscience.

The Three Beautiful Prayers help release people from their sins so that when the Day of Judgment comes, which is soon; souls will be ready for heaven.

Mom and I found out that when we pray for those who have died, some of the people do not answer. They are already in heaven or they still have to atone for their failure to worship. Some souls do not answer right away, but then later come to us and thank us. Sometimes we get an answer the next day, sometimes weeks or even months later. I will think of them for no reason and I'll usually think, "Why am I thinking of this person?" and they'll answer, "Because I am here to thank you for praying for me."

Then again, some people that we pray for stop us after the 1st or 2nd prayer and say, "Your prayers have already helped me when you said the Three Very Beautiful Prayers for me when I was still alive. Please stop praying that prayer and pray for my family." They are very adamant about it. We just don't realize how powerful prayer is, or how short time of our life remaining on earth is.

I remember exactly where I was when God gave me the revelation why the three prayers have to be said for the whole world. It was when I still had doubts about writing this book, and I didn't realize the significance of it all. I was walking into a Christian bookstore with my Mom and it just came to me. (It's like God opens up your head, puts the knowledge in and closes it back). Just like that—I turned to my Mom and said, "I know why these prayers have to be said for the whole world!" She replied, "What? Why?" I said, "God just told me, because these are the last days and judgment is near, people will not have time to spend in purgatory getting their soul right with God.

Talking to a spirit is just like having a conversation with God. It is a thought that comes into your mind that is not your own. Everyone has had guidance from God, the Holy Spirit, their guardian angel, or possibly even a loved one that has passed on. It's that little voice you hear sometimes, maybe telling you to take a different route to work and then you hear of a terrible accident that occurred on your usual route.

The closer you get to God, through prayer, meditation and studying His Word, the more aware you will become of the presence of the spiritual world.

"There is an active spirit world all around us, full of angels, demons, the Holy Spirit, the omnipresent Father, and His omnipresent Son, Jesus. The only reasons for me not to see this reality are unbelief or lack of knowledge." (Mark and Patti Virkler, "You Can Hear God's Voice")

Chapter Four

We Must Intercede for the Salvation of Souls

"He who saves souls is wise." (Proverbs 11:30)

"I urge, then first of all, that requests, prayers, intercession and thanksgiving be made for everyone—for kings and all those in authority, that we may live peaceful and quiet lives in all godliness and holiness. This is good, and pleases God our Savior, who wants all men to be saved and to come to knowledge of the truth." (1 Timothy 2:1-4)

My Mom grew up on a farm in Texas. There were 12 children in her family. When she was 13, she and her little sister, age 9, went across the farm to bring the milk cow home. They came around a curve in the road and found their Dad lying lifeless on the ground beside the tractor. He was 47 years old. Mom knew immediately that he was dead. This experience in her life brought her to the realization that there is life after death. She thought that if there really is a God, then she will see her Dad again. This is when she started to pray the rosary every day like the Nuns in Catholic School taught her.

"It is, therefore, a holy and wholesome thought to pray for the dead, that they may be loosed from sin." (2Macabees 12:46, the Catholic Bible)

When another relative of Mom's passed away, she decided to pray an extra rosary every day for a year for her soul. The Nuns always talked about purgatory and Mom wanted her relative to be with her Dad in heaven.

Soon, Mom had people who died asking her for prayer. In 1984, when she was forty years old, she received a letter in the mail that had "Elvis Fan Club" printed on the envelope. She thought, "I'm a little too old to be invited to join a fan club." As she opened the letter she got cold chills from head to toe. Then Elvis spoke to her saying,

"Please pray two rosaries a day for a year for me so that I can enter heaven." Mom thought she was daydreaming or imagining this and dismissed it from her mind. "How could Elvis talk to me?" she thought. Then, he asked her again, this time ending with, "Please do it!" She decided to do it, and on the last day she was very busy and did not get the rosaries said until late that night. Just as she finished, Elvis spoke to her saying, "I've been waiting all day. This is the longest day I ever had. Thank you for praying for me. I can't thank you enough. Thank you! Thank you Very Much!"

The spirits are searching for people to pray for them to help release them of their sins. **If we fail to worship God and repent of our sins here on earth, then we will have to atone for our sins after we die.**

Jesus said, "I am the way and the truth and the life. No one comes to the Father except through me." (John 14:6). If we do not accept Jesus Christ as our Lord and Savior and surrender our lives to Him, we will not enter heaven. This is the only way.

God created us to share our life with Him. "For by Him all things were created: things in heaven and on earth, visible and invisible, whether thrones or powers or rulers or authorities, all things were created by Him and for Him." (Col. 1:16)

If a person does not know God because they are not praying and including God in their life, then someone has to intercede for them or they will not go to heaven.

God loves to hear from us. He loves to help us. We must humble ourselves and "come near to God and He will come near to you." (James 4:8)

I believe this is why He revealed to us the power of the "Three Very Beautiful Prayers", as the end of time is drawing near. "Blessed is the one who reads the words of this prophecy, and blessed are those who hear it and take to heart what is written in it, because the time is near." (Revelations 1:3)

We no longer have time to pray rosaries every day for years for our loved ones to enter heaven. To help release souls of their sins, you should recite the "Three Very Beautiful Prayers".

Now, this doesn't mean you can live your life as you please, sinning and disobeying God's commandments, and then say the prayers and you will go to heaven. We have learned through praying for so many souls that some souls, who never worshipped God and lived their lives following their own selfish desires, did not get released into heaven (forgiven of their sins) right away. Even after prayer, some still have to suffer and worship God until their heart is right.

First of all, you must accept Jesus Christ as your Lord and Savior. If you reject Him, this is an unforgivable sin. No amount of praying can save you. "Whoever believes in the Son has eternal life, but whoever rejects the Son will not see life, for God's wrath remains on him." (John 3:36). But, if you've tried to live your life the best you can, being kind to others, etc., the "Three Very Beautiful Prayers" does help, as you can see in the following story:

One the first people my Mom prayed for was her brother who died in 1969 at the age of 16. She wanted to talk to him so she read the three prayers and got no answer. She knew he was a nice person, so she read it again, and then once more. Then her brother spoke to her and said, "I cannot talk to you; I have to go worship at the throne." He explained, "**You have to answer to God for what you did wrong, and for what you failed to do.**" So Mom asked him, "Do I need to pray for you while you are at the throne worshipping?"

He said, "No, there is no way I will fail to worship God and leave this wonderful place!"

Another example is when my Mom prayed for a man that she knew most of her life, who we shall call Sam for privacy sake. He said, **"Thank you for praying for me. At least now my thirst has been quenched**. Please pray for my wife."

Then, when she prayed for another local man that passed away, he said, "I am up here with Sam for eternity because **I rejected Jesus too many times by not attending Church. We are very happy but we did not earn as many privileges and blessings as some people up here have."**

Now, don't get the misunderstanding that attending Church gets you into heaven. This man failed to worship God and that was his main sin. "In every lost person, there is one particular issue that stands between that person and God. For example, Jesus said to the rich young ruler, 'One thing thou lacks'. Greed was the issue. Jesus confronted the woman at the well with the issue of living in adultery. This issue was the stronghold the devil used to blind her mind to the gospel." (Praying Effectively for the Lost, Pg. 27)

"And even if our gospel is veiled, it is veiled to those who are perishing. The god of this age has blinded the minds of unbelievers so that they cannot see the light of the gospel of the glory of Christ, who is the image of God." (2Cor. 4:3-4)

I hear of people, who are blinded into thinking that they can live as they please, and they think that as long as they go to church on Sunday and regularly confess their sins to the priest and they will go to heaven. I love what Joyce Meyer says about it, "I can go sit in my garage but that doesn't make me a car." In other words, going to church doesn't make you a Christian. A Christian is, "one who professes belief in the teachings of Jesus Christ." (Webster's Collegiate Dictionary, 10th Edition) "It is an apt title for those 'belonging to Christ'." (NIV Study Bible)

A Christian tries to imitate Christ in their actions. It's not that you won't sin again, because we are all sinners and fall into temptation of the enemy. But, God knows our hearts and if we are truly sorry, and repent, then we are forgiven.

When you are truly a "born again" Christian, you have surrendered your life to Christ.

You no longer worry about things of this world; you no longer try to do anything on your own. You choose the Lord's Will over your own. If you are born again you will not desire your old life of sin.

"Those who live according to the sinful nature have their minds set on what the nature desires; but those who live in accordance with the Spirit have their minds set on what the Spirit desires . . . the sinful mind is hostile to God. It does not submit to God's law, nor can it do so. Those controlled by the sinful nature cannot please God. You however, are controlled not by the sinful nature but by the Spirit, if the Spirit of God lives in you." (Romans 8:5-9)

"Peter began to speak: I now realize how true it is that God does not show favoritism but accepts man from every nation who fear Him and do what is right." (Acts 10:34-35)

My Mom prayed for someone who said, "You just sit there showing no emotion. You don't realize what you just did for me. I must tell you it is so glorious!"

We must all come to know God and surrender our lives to Him before we can enter heaven. Some people surrender their lives to God without having to go through all the trials and sufferings. The rest of us, for some reason, do not search for and find God until we have hard times, or in my case—great suffering and persecution.

The Bible says "We must go through many hardships to enter the kingdom of God." (Acts 14:22) And, "Blessed is the man who perseveres under trial, because when he has stood the test, he will receive the crown of life that God has promised to those who love Him." (James 1:12)

So what happens to those who die before they know God? **They need prayer!** They are doing their suffering in purgatory. Prayer shortens that time. Remember 'Sam'? After my Mom prayed for him he thanked her and said, "At least now my thirst has been quenched." My Mom was worried about his salvation because he lived a reckless life (for lack of a better term), not to be judgmental but some people we can discern whether they are Christians or not by the way they live their lives. So she asked God why He took Sam's life at a fairly young age before he had surrendered it to Him. God told her He had to take his life to save his soul. God said, **"The longer he lived on earth, the more of his soul he lost to the devil. In his daily life, his evil works outweighed his good works."** Wow! This was a new revelation for us.

The longer he lived on earth, the more of his soul he lost to the devil. Remember his friend said, "We have not earned as many blessings as others have." Sam lived his life for himself, not for God, but because someone prayed for his salvation, God did what He had to do for Sam to be saved. If nobody had prayed for Sam, God would have left him alone because God gives us a free will, and he wouldn't have gone to heaven.

"Just as Isaiah prophesied, 'The Lord has blinded their eyes and deadened their hearts, so they can neither see with their eyes, nor understand with their hearts, nor turn—and I would heal them.' For they loved praise from men more than praise from God. Even after Jesus had done miraculous signs in their presence, they still would not believe in Him." (John 12:37, 40, 43)

God does not interfere with our free will. He knows our hearts, and he knows if we are going to surrender to Him or not. If NOT, then there is nothing more He can do to help us. Just as Paul states in 2Thessalonians 2:10-12 "They perish because they refused to love the truth and so be saved." For this reason God sends a powerful delusion so that they will believe the lie and so that all will be condemned who have not believed the truth but have delighted in wickedness."

If we want our loved ones who do not know God to be in heaven with us for eternity, then we must intercede for them. **Salvation**

of souls is the only thing that matters. Even after we die we will be helping guide souls to Christ.

Steve Erwin's passion on earth was saving God's creatures. He taught us to love through his love for all living things. Now in his spirit life, his passion has turned toward the salvation of souls. After I prayed for him he asked me to pray for his loved ones—after saying WOO HOO all day! He came back to me many times asking me to say the Three Very Beautiful Prayers for the souls in Australia. **I asked him why Australia needs so many prayers—more than other countries. He said that this is something he can do for his people now to make up for what he failed to do when he was alive.**

Never give up! "The Lord richly blesses all who call on HIM." (Romans 10:12). If miracles don't happen in your life, you only have the word of God in your mind, not in your heart.

"It is important to be persistent in prayer." (Matt 7:7-8)

Just look at how God has blessed me and my Mom for saying the salvation prayers over and over. When we first started saying them, we didn't know if they were working or not. We just kept saying them and all of a sudden, we have spirits, those who have died, helping us because we helped them. "We live by faith, not by sight." (2Co 5:7)

My Mom was listening to Tammy Wynette's music and Tammy spoke to her, "I'm glad you like my music. I'm trying to help you since you prayed the salvation prayers for me, but **I can only**

help you a little because I suffered a lot in my life and saved myself mostly."

I wasn't going to include this in the book until I was watching the Kennedy Center Honors and when they were honoring George Jones, I got goose bumps from head to toe. I thought, "Wow! This must be Tammy Wynette." (I thought this because she had just recently talked to my Mom). When they were singing his songs and put the camera on George, Tammy said, "I love him." When they sang another of his songs, Tammy said, "I always loved it when George sang that to me."

When I sat down to write that night I got goose bumps again and Tammy said, "Please write what I said in the book."

God does answer prayer! And, when you ask for something for His greater glory—He answers on the divine level! In other words, if we ask for something that will better His kingdom, He will give you a supernatural answer.

My Mom prayed the three prayers for members of the Joe Kennedy family. One day she was watching a documentary on President John F. Kennedy. A spirit communicated to her, "Thank you for praying for my family." Mom asked, "Is this the President I am speaking to?" He said, "Yes. I didn't get justice when I was on earth. I am going to see that you get justice." Mom asked, "While I'm still alive?" He answered, "Yes!"

Marilyn Monroe said to my Mom, "Tell Johnson not to believe what people are saying. He knows the truth."

"God is able to do immeasurably more than all we ask or imagine, according to his power that is at work within us." (Eph. 3:20)

"Commit your way to the Lord, trust in Him and He will do this: He will make your righteousness shine like the dawn, the justice of your cause like the noonday sun." (Psalms 37:5-7)

"No eye has seen, no ear has heard, no mind has conceived what God has prepared for those who love him. But God has revealed it to us by His Spirit." (1Cor. 2:9-10)

Chapter Five

We Feel Their Emotions

"And pray in the Spirit on all occasions with all kinds of prayers and requests. With this in mind, be alert and always keep on praying for all the saints." (Ephesians 6:18)

With this new revelation from God, Mom and I started praying for everyone who died. We prayed for all the local obituaries in the papers, plus all names we heard announced on TV. We started to learn what happens to people when they die.

All my life I've heard, "God takes the good people." It was just something people always say at a funeral to make their loved ones feel better, I guess. So I used to think I don't want to live my life 'spiritually perfect' because I don't want to die yet. That was when I still feared death. But God has taught me to not fear anything of this world, only Him.

"You alone are to be feared." ((Psalms 76:7)

"The fear of the Lord is the beginning of knowledge, but fools despise wisdom and discipline." (Proverbs 1:7)

"Through the fear of the Lord a man avoids evil." (Proverbs 16:6)

"Fear of man will prove to be a snare, but whoever trusts in the Lord is kept safe." (Proverbs 29:25)

"The fear of the Lord leads to life. Then one rests content, untouched by trouble." (Proverbs 19:23)

When God awakens me at 3:00 a.m. and tells me to write, it is through fear of Him that I obey. The words flow freely on the paper when I write when He tells me to. When I try to do it on my own, nothing comes to me.

I know that if I don't do His Will, I will not receive all the blessings He has for me.

Blessings for obedience (Duet. 28:1-14) "If you obey the Lord your God and carefully follow all his commands I give you today, the Lord will set you high above all the nations on earth. All these blessings will come to you and accompany you if you obey the Lord your God:

You will be blessed in the city and blessed in the country.

The fruit of your womb will be blessed, and the crops of your land and the young of your livestock—the calves of your herds and the lambs of your flocks.

Your basket (food) and your kneading trough will be blessed.

You will be blessed when you come in and when you go out.

The Lord will grant that the enemies who rise up against you will be defeated before you. They will come at you from one direction and flee from you in seven.

The Lord will establish you as his holy people, as he promised you on oath if you keep the command of the Lord your God and walk in his ways. Then all the people on earth will see that you are called by the name of the Lord, and they will fear you. The Lord will grant you abundant prosperity—in the fruit of your womb, the young of your livestock and the crops of your ground—in the land he swore to your forefathers to give to you.

The Lord will open the heavens, the storehouse of his bounty, to send rain on your land in season and to bless all the work of your hands. You will lend to many nations but will borrow from none. The Lord will make you the head, not the tail. If you pay attention to the commands of the Lord your God that I give you this day and carefully follow them, you will always be at the top, never at the bottom. Do not turn aside from any of the commands I give you today, to the right or to the left, following other gods or serving them."

WOW! And the 'Curses for Disobedience' (Deut. 28:15-69) are more than three times this long.

You may think that your loved ones when they die are 'finally at peace', 'in a better place', or 'feel no more pain', but that is not the case for everyone. Mom and I have learned that, upon death, **no one enters heaven until they are spiritually perfect.** They remain in a state of 'limbo', 'purgatory', or whatever you may call it, to atone for their sins and to prove to God that they love Him above all else.

Most of the dead feel great sorrow for their sins. I have had many of the people that I know that I prayed for tell me they were sorry over and over. I would say, "For what?"

They answer, "For treating you the way I did." When I prayed fot a lady that I personally knew, I immediately started bawling uncontrollably. It was her emotions I was feeling because I wasn't sad about anything when I started praying for her. She told me she was sorry over and over and I thought to myself, "Why?" She said, "For the way my family is treating you."

This lady did not go to heaven right away when she died. She had to make amends for her sins. And because my prayers helped her, she was able to help me, and she wanted to help me.

My Mom prayed for one of her former teacher's and then asked her for advice. Her teacher said, **"I'm already in heaven. I'm not allowed to talk to you."**

Mr. Don Piper experienced heaven personally and lived to tell about it in his book, "90 Minutes in Heaven". He says, "I wasn't conscious of anything I'd left behind and felt no regrets about leaving my family or possessions. It was as if God had removed anything negative or worrisome from my consciousness." (Pg. 26) "Being separated from my family had never crossed my mind while I was in heaven. People in heaven simply don't have an awareness of who is not there. (Pg. 203)

So those who have spiritual perfection, attained by daily prayers for forgiveness of their sins or martyrdom, go straight to heaven when they die. Others have to atone for their sins in purgatory. They have to either worship at the throne or help guide others to heaven. These souls still feel pain and sorrow and miss their loved ones who are alive on earth.

When I heard Johnny Cash died, I prayed for him. I was out walking doing my praying and as soon as I finished the last line of the three prayers, I felt great joy and got goose bumps all over, and then he said, "Thank you so much." Not realizing what I just heard, not believing that I was talking to Johnny Cash, I continued praying. He said thank you again, then he said, "I don't know you." I thought, "I know you and I just pray for everyone that I hear has died."

I felt his presence with me for a couple of days. In other words, I kept thinking about him on and off for no particular reason. A spirit will do that to get your attention, their name comes to your mind and you don't know why. Or, when you think of them first, you will get a sign like goose bumps or your hair will stand on end. Mom and I finally figured out that they stay with us to get us to pray the "Open Heart and Mind Prayer" for their loved ones, or they are with us to help guide and comfort us as a favor in return for our prayers releasing them from their sins. I can't even count the times I felt alone that I would hear, "I'm here!" or "We're here!" and then their names would come to mind immediately after. The love I feel from them is indescribable. They don't have the devil holding them back from showing or feeling the love that we all have been given from God.

When I watched the movie, "I Walk the Line" about Johnny Cash, I cried and cried. It wasn't my emotion, it was his. It came to me that he is sad for his family and friends and misses them very much. He asked me to pray for them.

While walking one day I prayed for a local man who had just died and I immediately started crying uncontrollably. I cannot control it because the spirit is giving me the emotion. If I stop thinking about that person I could stop crying, but I wanted to know why he was so sad and I wanted to help him. I had to tell him to stop crying so I could continue praying. He was in great sorrow for his family and wanted me to pray for them. I was curious what they could be doing that brought their loved one such sorrow, but he could not tell me that. That is none of my business and we are only accountable to God for our own sins. God has called me to pray for the salvation of souls and that is all that matters.

The Spirit of God has given me the strong desire to save souls. Once I became born again, all I wanted was to tell the world of this wonderful truth that will set them free. I am sure everyone who receives the Spirit of God feels the same. Such was Paul's great love for his fellow Jews in Romans 9:2-3, "I have great sorrow and unceasing anguish in my heart, for I wish that I myself were cursed and cut off from Christ for the sake of my brothers." And Moses in Exodus 32:31-32, "So Moses went back to the Lord and said, 'Oh what a great sin these people have committed! They have made themselves gods of gold.' But now, please forgive their sin—but if not, then blot me out of the book you have written. (Moses' gracious offer is refused because the person who sins is responsible for his own sin.)"

"My commandment is this: Love one another as I have loved you. Greater love has no one than this—that he lay down his life for his friends." (John 15:12-13)

Rev. Lee E. Thomas talks about going to hell for another in his book, "Praying Effective for the Lost". He said, "When I was teaching a seminary extension class on Personal Evangelism, I printed up some prayer list cards with the inscription, 'I'll go to Hell for you'. The idea was to list the names of people for whom we would be willing to go to hell in their stead and pray accordingly. At the next class meeting, after having distributed the cards to my students, one of them, a pastor, said, 'I don't think I am willing to go to hell for anyone.' He pretty much spoke for all of us. Although God would not allow for us to take another's place in hell, it sure would increase the effectiveness of our prayers for them if we were so willing."

When I read this I thought, "I'd go to hell for anyone and everyone." I wish it were that easy to save souls.

"To be humble means to truly love people to the point of being willing to die for them. 'Humble' means we think more of others than ourselves." (Marie Chapian, Angels in Our Lives)

"Do nothing out of selfish ambition or vain conceit, but in humility consider others better than yourself. Each of you should look not only to your own interest, but also to the interests of others. Your attitude should be the same as that of Christ Jesus: Who being in very nature God, did not consider equality with God something to be grasped, but made himself nothing, taking the very nature of a servant, being made in human likeness. Jesus humbled himself and became obedient to death—even death on a cross!" (Philippians 2:3-8)

Chapter Six

Achieving Eternal Life with God

"See that what you have learned from the beginning remains in you. I am writing these things to you about those who are trying to lead you astray. As for you, the anointing you received from Him remains in you, and you do not need anyone to teach you." (1John 2:24, 26-27)

Being able to talk to the spirits is a supernatural blessing, a gift from God, an answer to my prayers because I was "seeking with all my heart". (Heb. 11:6; Jeremiah. 29:12-14)

Every time it happens I am WOWED! I still can't believe it is happening to me, and why? When I ask them why, they say so nonchalantly, "Because you prayed for us."

There is so much more happening in the spirit, that we cannot see, than what is happening in our carnal world, that we can see. So when you are persecuted, "Do not lose heart". What is happening to your spirit is so much more important than what is happening in the world. What happens to our physical bodies is temporary, but what happens to our spirit is eternal.

"Therefore we do not lose heart. Though outwardly we are wasting away, yet inwardly we are being renewed day by day. For, our light and momentary troubles are achieving for us an eternal glory that far outweighs them all. So we fix our eyes not on what is seen, but on what is unseen. For what is seen is temporary, but what is unseen is eternal." (2Cor. 4:16-17)

Paul says not to fix our eyes on things of this world because this world is only temporary. Our time here is so minute compared to eternal life with God. **But every second on this earth matters**. Every single thought you have matters.

Everything Matters! If all you have is negative thoughts, evil thoughts, thoughts of hatred toward others, then your soul is being lost to the devil because everything evil is of the devil.

The Apostle Peter warns us in 1Peter 2:11, "Dear friends, I urge you to abstain your sinful desires, which war against your soul." **Jesus says, "What good will it be for a man if he gains the whole world, yet forfeits his soul?"** (Matt. 16:26)

Everything you do either brightens your soul and you gain more blessings from heaven, or it will darken your soul and you sell a little more of it to the devil, with your blessings held back.

My Mom was watching a Jesse James movie and she felt that she should pray for him to be saved. When she finished the three prayers, he said to her, "I cannot believe that I am finally released from my sins. I waited so long and I am prayed for by the most beautiful woman I have ever seen." Mom said, "I am not beautiful." He said, **"We see your soul. It is very beautiful! It is very bright!"**

The most obvious way to lose your soul to the devil, of course, is breaking any of the Ten Commandments of God handed down to Moses. Thou shalt not steal, commit murder, commit adultery, and covet, and so on. But did you ever stop to think about the little things we do everyday that the devil is tempting us to do, that darkens our soul little by little. Every unkind word, mean look, stare or glare, and especially gossip. Christ is not in us when we say anything mean about anybody.

"A fool's mouth is his undoing, and his lips are a snare to his soul." (Proverbs 18:7)

"If anyone considers himself religious and yet does not keep a tight rein on his tongue, he deceives himself and his religion is worthless." (James 1:26) Gossiping—slandering someone's name—is cursing them. When you curse others you may think at the time that you are hurting them, but are only hurting yourself and God. **God says, "I will bless those who bless you, and whoever curses you I will curse**." (Gen.12:3)

"Bless those who persecute you, bless and do not curse." (Romans 12:14)

Just as the persecutor's soul darkens, the Christian's soul, (who endures and overcomes), gets brighter. Jesus spoke, "I am the light of the world. Whoever follows me will never walk in darkness, but will have the light of life." (John 8:12)

We must even keep our thoughts pure. Every evil thing spoke or acted upon first began with a thought that the devil puts in our minds. It only becomes a sin if you dwell on or act upon that thought. If you dwell on evil thoughts you darken your soul. To brighten our souls we must do as stated in (Phil. 4:8-9). "Fill your mind and meditate on whatever is true, whatever is noble, whatever is right, whatever is pure, whatever is lovely, whatever is admirable—if anything is excellent or praiseworthy—think about such things."

We must only look for the good in everything and everybody. A sin isn't just a sin when you do the action. You are sinning if you are just thinking about it. It is a sin if you think about yourself with another's spouse—that's adultery. If you just think about wishing someone was dead—that's murder.

Do not be deceived. Do not fall into the devil's trap of lies. If something doesn't sound quite right, then more likely it is not. "The devil is the author of confusion and Jesus is the author of peace." (Rev. James Robinson)

"Woe (great sorrow, grief and misery) to those who call evil good and good evil."
(Isaiah 5:20)

"You weary the Lord with your words by saying, 'all who do evil are good in the eyes of the Lord, and he is pleased with them'." (Malachi 2:17)

The Bible warns us "I urge you, brothers, to watch out for those who cause divisions and put obstacles in your way that are contrary to the teaching you have learned. Keep away from them. For such people are not serving our Lord Christ, but their own appetites. By smooth talk and flattery they deceive the minds of naïve people. Be wise about what is good." (Romans 16:17-18)

Listen to your first instinct. God will tell us what is the truth—usually only once. He doesn't get in the way of our own free will. Then the devil will try to confuse us.

You are not following Christ and doing God's Will if you are not showing love to one another. This is done through acts of kindness just as Jesus showed us during His time on earth.

"A new command I give you: Love one another as I have loved you." (John 13:34)

"The commandments, 'Do not commit adultery', 'Do not murder", Do not steal', Do not covet', and whatever other commandments there may be, are summed up in this one rule: **'Love your neighbor as yourself.'** Love does no harm to its neighbor. Therefore love is the fulfillment of the law." (Romans 13:9-10)

"But I tell you, love your enemies and pray for those who persecute you." (Matthew 5:44)

When I first personally witnessed people being mean and hateful, it broke my heart and crushed my spirit. For the first time in my life I was experiencing a broken heart and I was so surprised that you can physically feel it. The pain and anguish I felt in my chest was unbearable.

I felt betrayed by every single person I knew. The only one I could turn to was God. I kept asking, "Why?" The movie, The Passion, came out at this time and I could really relate to Jesus' persecution. There is no reason for it. It is unreasonable. It is "treacherous (unfaithfulness, disloyalty, betrayal) without excuse". (Psalms 25:3)

One night while praying outside, I was asking God, "Why?" I was crying and shaking from the cold and all of a sudden a warm sensation went from the top of my head down to my feet. I was silenced in wonder. Just then Jesus spoke to me so plain, **"They are not doing it to you, they are doing it to Me."**

"If the world hates you, keep in mind that it hated me first. If you belonged to the world, it would love you as its own. As it is, you do not belong to the world, but I have chosen you out of the world. That is why the world hates you. If they persecuted me, they will persecute you also. They will treat you this way because of my name, for they do not know the one who sent me." (John 15:18-21)

We should not **HATE** anyone. **Man is not our enemy**. The world is not man against man. It is the devil against God. Man just falls under the temptation of the devil. So we should only hate what man does to us, but should not hate man. Man is created in God's image. We are all equal in the eyes of God. This is the revelation that helped me to forgive! It is not personal! If someone is mean they are under control of the devil. This is why Jesus said to pray for and bless those who persecute us! We are all sinners. "For all have sinned and fall short of the glory of God." (Romans 3:23). We all fall under the temptation of the devil at one time or another!

"Anyone who claims to be in the light but hates his brother is still in darkness." (1John 2-9)

"Do not be overcome by evil, but overcome evil with good."(Romans 12:21). If you do evil to get your own revenge or justice, then you are falling under the temptation of the devil just as your enemy. Instead, we must pray for our enemy. We cannot change people, but God can!

"Do not take revenge, my friends, but leave room for God's wrath, for it is written: 'It is mine to avenge; I will repay', says the Lord. On the contrary: If your enemy is hungry, feed him; if he is thirsty, give him something to drink. In doing this, you will heap burning coals on his head." (Romans 12:19-20). "Do not follow the ruler of the kingdom of the air, the spirit who is at work in those who are disobedient." (Eph. 2:2)

"This is what the Lord says: cursed is the one who trusts in man, who depends on flesh for his strength and whose heart turns away from the Lord. I, the Lord search the heart and examine the mind, to reward a man according to his conduct, according to what his deeds deserve." (Jer.17:5)

"Put on the full armor of God so that you can take your stand against the devil's schemes. For our struggle is not against flesh and blood, but against the rulers, against the authorities, against the powers of the dark world and against the spiritual forces of evil in the heavenly realms." (Eph. 6:11-12)

"If anyone says, 'I love God', yet hates his brother, he is a liar. For anyone who does not love his brother, whom he has seen, cannot love God, whom he has not seen. And he has given us this command: whoever loves God must also love his brother." (1John 4:20-21)

"It is better to take refuge in the Lord than to trust in man." (Psalms 118:8)

"Dear friend, do not imitate what is evil but what is good. Anyone who does what is good is from God. Anyone who does what is evil has not seen God." (3John 1:11)

"Do not plot evil against your neighbor, I hate this, declares the Lord." (Zech. 8:17)

"If a man pays back evil for good, evil will never leave his house." (Proverbs 17:13)

If you have to do anything in secret—you shouldn't be doing it. You should have nothing to hide if you are living God's Will.

"Have nothing to do with the fruitless deeds of darkness, but rather expose them. For it is shameful even to mention what the disobedient do in secret." (Eph. 5:11)

"Woe to those who go to great depths to hide their plans from the Lord, who do their work in darkness and think: Who sees us? Who will know"? (Isaiah 29:15)

One day, my Mom was resting after a long day of work and she suddenly felt sad and tears welled up in her eyes. The, she cried and cried. She said she hardly ever cries. She didn't know what she was crying about. She questioned the spirits who were making her feel so sad. They said to her, **"You don't know how much it hurts to look down to earth and see that your family will not be with you in heaven for eternity."**

I personally know only a few of the things that the disobedient do in secret which God revealed to me and my Mom through prayer. The little I know about breaks my heart; I can't even imagine what our loved ones who have passed on are witnessing. They tell me that they wish their loved ones knew the truth that I know. All I can say is—it's in the Bible. I love the song that says, "It is no secret what God can do, what He's done for others, He'll do for you!"

"Jesus said, 'do not be afraid of them. **There is nothing concealed that will not be disclosed, or hidden that will not be made known.** Do not be afraid of those who kill the body but cannot kill the soul'." (Matthew 10:26-28)

"Do not be deceived: God cannot be mocked. A man reaps what he sows. The one who sows to please his sinful nature, from that nature will reap destruction; the one who sows to please the spirit, from the spirit will reap eternal life." (Gal. 6:7-8)

Do not think that you are getting away with anything that you do in secret. God sees everything!

"If a man digs a pit, he will fall into it. (The trouble he causes will recoil on himself)."

(Proverbs 26:27, NIV KJ Study Bible)

"The Lord says, 'My eyes are on all their ways, they are not hidden from me, nor is their sin concealed from my eyes. **I will repay them double for their wickedness and their sin**, because they have defiled my land with the lifeless forms of their vile images and have filled my inheritance with their detestable idols'." (Jeremiah 16:17-18)

"This is the verdict: Light has come into the world, but men loved darkness instead of light because their deeds were evil. Everyone who does evil hates the light, and will not come into the light for fear that his deeds will be exposed. But whoever lives by the truth comes into the light, so that it may be seen plainly that what he has done has been done through God." (John 3:19-21)

"Turn to Me and be saved, all you ends of the earth, for I am God and there is no other."
(Isaiah 45:22)

Chapter Seven

The End is Near

"You must be ready, because the Son of Man will come at an hour when you do not expect him." (Luke 12:40)

"The day of the Lord is near for all nations. As you have done, it will be done to you; your deeds will return upon your own head." (Obadiah 15)

"But mark this: There will be terrible times in the last days. People will be lovers of themselves, lovers of money, boastful, proud, abusive, disobedient to their parents, ungrateful, unholy, without love, unforgiving, slanderous, without self control, brutal, not lovers of the good, treacherous, rash, and conceited, lovers of pleasure rather than lovers of God—having a form of godliness but denying its power. Have nothing to do with them." (2 Timothy 3:1-5)

This time of our lives is a test. God is testing us to see if we will choose Him or the world. "The testing of your faith produces patience. But let patience have its perfect work, that you may be perfect and complete, not lacking in anything." (James 1:3-4)

We pass the test by reacting to situations according to God's Word. If we meet someone on the street and show them kindness, we are blessed accordingly—"You reap what you sow". (Gal. 6:7). If you are mean, then "As I have observed, those who plow evil and those who sow trouble reap it. At the breath of God they are destroyed." (Job 4:8)

We must always stay positive in good times and bad. If we are strong in our faith and choose God when times are bad, verses choosing evil, which is much easier, then we will have eternal life. **"Be faithful, even to the point of death, and I will give you the crown of life."** (Revelation 2:10)

What happens to us is not as important as our reaction to what happens to us. "Though now for a little while you may have had to suffer grief in all kinds of trials. These have come so that your faith—of greater worth than gold—may be proved genuine and may result in praise, glory and honor when Jesus Christ is revealed." (1Peter 1:6-7)

Every single thing that happens to us in life brings us closer to where God wants us to be. Every accident, disaster, win or loss, every person we meet—even if it's just a second on the street—every little thing happens for a reason. "There are no coincidences." (Oprah Winfrey)

Do Not Judge

"Here there is no Greek or Jew, slave or free, but Christ is all, and is in all." (Col. 3:11)

When my Mom prayed for Sadaam Hussein he answered her right away. He said, "Please pray for the Iraqi people."

When Mom told me this I was shocked. The world had made him out to be a horrible terrorist, but he was just doing what he had to do as a leader, what he thought he had to do to protect his people.

We do not know the heart of another, only God knows. "For who among men knows the thoughts of a man except the man's spirit within him?" (1Cor. 2:11)

We must stop judging each other because we are all the same. On Judgment Day when you stand before Almighty God, you will only have to answer for yourself. "Each of us will give an account of himself to God. Therefore let us stop passing judgment on one another. Instead, make up your mind not to put any stumbling block or obstacle in your brother's way." (Romans 14:11-13)

"Do not judge, and you will not be judged. Do not condemn, and you will not be condemned. Forgive, and you will be forgiven. Give, and it will be given to you. For with the measure you use, it will be measured to you." (Luke 6:37-38)

"Why do you look at the speck of sawdust in your brother's eye and pay no attention to the plank in your own eye?" (Luke 6:42). We should not be foolish and hypocritical by criticizing someone else's fault while failing to see our own substantial faults.

No Reason to Doubt

We have no reason to doubt and not believe in God. He has revealed Himself to the world. He has given us all a chance to surrender to Him. "Consequently, faith comes from hearing the message, and the message is heard through the word of Christ. But I ask: Did they not hear? Of course they did. 'Their voice has gone out into all the earth, their words to the ends of the world." (Romans 10:17-18)

"No one—not even one who has not heard of the Bible or of Christ—has an excuse for not honoring God, because the whole created world reveals Him." (NIV Study Bible, Pg. 1708)

"The wrath of God is being revealed from heaven against all the godlessness and wickedness of men who suppress the truth by their wickedness, since what may be known about God is plain to them, because God has made it plain to them. For since the creation of the world God's invisible qualities—his eternal power and divine nature—have been clearly seen, being understood from what has been made, so that men are without excuse." (Romans 1:18-20)

To anyone who doubts there even is a God, that there really is a heaven and a hell, I recommend reading '90 Minutes in Heaven', by Don Piper and '23 Minutes in Hell', by Bill Wiese.

"Do not believe every spirit, but test the spirits to see whether they are from God, because many false prophets have gone out into the world. This is how you can recognize the Spirit of God. Every spirit that acknowledges that Jesus Christ has come in the flesh is from God, but every spirit that does not acknowledge Jesus is not from God. This is the spirit of the antichrist, which you have heard is coming and even now is already in the world." (1John 4:1-3)

Chapter Eight

Salvation Lies in Repentance and Rebirth in Christ

God wants us all to live eternally with Him. "He is patient with you, not wanting anyone to perish, but everyone to come to repentance." (2Peter 3:9)

"This is what the sovereign Lord, the Holy One of Israel, says, 'In repentance and rest is your salvation, in quietness and trust is your strength'." (Isaiah 30:15)

"Jesus declared, 'I tell you the truth, no one can see the kingdom of God unless he is born again." (John 3:3)

We will all die sooner or later, leave this world and go on to a better place, we hope, and pray? In the past, if a person died before they were born again, they had time to worship God in purgatory, to show their love for Him and make up for their sins. Now, there is no time. We all know the end of the world is very soon! So, if we want to be saved, we must surrender now, while still alive. Stop living a selfish life of sin—and repent.

Armageddon is it! That's Judgment Day! If you haven't repented from sin and accepted Jesus in your life by then, that's it. When you die, that death is for eternity. You can only have eternal life if you know Jesus.

"I am the way and the truth and the life. No one comes to the Father except through me." (John 14:6)

I understand why some people are afraid to die. If they don't know Jesus Christ, and they die, then they will not be resurrected to life eternal. They know where they are going. Personally, I've been ready to die the day I was born again. When you give your life to Christ, he reveals the truth to you and you are not afraid to die.

"There is no fear in love. Perfect love drives out fear, because fear has to do with punishment. The one who fears is not made perfect in love. **God is love**." (1John 4:16-18)

We are all going to die from this world, but your goal should be to go to heaven and have eternal life with God. If you surrender your life to Jesus, die to self now and become born again (new life in Christ), then your eternal life with Him is secure.

To be born again doesn't mean you can't have any fun any more. You can still go out and have a good time, it's just different. Instead of gossiping about others, tell something funny that you did. Learn to laugh at yourself, instead of others. Buy a dinner and a drink for a homeless guy on the street and you'll enjoy yours much more. When your conscience is clean, you

feel the joy of the Lord. Life is fun in a better way, God's way.

"O Jesus! Mirror of eternal splendor! Remember the sadness which Thou experienced when, contemplating in the light of Thy Divinity the predestination of those who would be saved by the merits of Thy Sacred Passion, Thou didst see at the same time, the great multitude of reprobates who would be damned for their sins, and Thou didst complain bitterly of those hopeless, lost and unfortunate sinners." (Pieta Prayer Book, St Bridget 15 Prayers, Prayer 5)

"Repent! Turn away from all your offenses, and then sin will not be your downfall. Rid yourselves of all the offenses you have committed and get a new heart and a new spirit.

For I take no pleasure in the death of anyone, declares the Sovereign Lord. Repent and live!" (Ezek. 18:30-32)

How can one be saved? Repentance is turning from sin, and faith is turning to God. **After you repent, you must trust the Lord and His Word.** Know His Word and believe it. When he says, "If a wicked man turns away from all the sins he has committed and keeps all my decrees (Ten Commandments) and does what is just, he will surely live, he will not die. None of the offenses he has committed will be remembered against him." (Ezek. 18:21-22)

Believe Him! Do not trust in the voice who tells you, "You might as well keep on doing what you're doing because you are going to hell anyway." That is a lie! Know God's word and believe it!

You can have eternal life no matter what you did in the past. God said so.

Billy Graham says to 'take God's word literally'. You have to know God's word or you will be easily deceived.

"In God, whose word I praise, in God I trust, I will not be afraid. What can mortal man do to me?" (Psalms 56:4)

Repentance is a change of mind and will, arising from sorrow for sin and leading to transformation of life.

"Repent, then, and turn to God, so that your sins may be wiped out, that times of refreshing may come from the Lord." (Acts 3:19)

Once you are born again, accept the Holy Spirit in your life, God will begin to convict you. You will not be able to go on sinning. The Holy Spirit guides you through your conscience. Personally, I cried every day. It hurts like hell to come to the realization of your sins. **But, we have to go through that to get to the glory!**

Remember, when the end of the world comes, that's it! There will be no second chances. That is Judgment Day! Listen to God's word. "The soul who sins is the one who will die. The son will not share the guilt of the father, nor will the father share the guilt of the son. The righteousness of the righteous man will be credited to him, and the wickedness of the wicked will be charged against him." (Ezek. 18:20). It may sound harsh, but it is true. **The sooner you repent, the better**. It takes time for your faith, knowledge and love of God to grow. Do not procrastinate! We do not know the day or the hour of Christ's coming!

"No one knows about that day or hour, not even the angels in heaven, nor the Son, but only the Father. As it was in the days of Noah, so it will be at the coming of the Son of Man. For in the days before the flood, people were eating and drinking . . . up to the day Noah entered the ark; and they knew nothing about what would happen until the flood came and took them all away. That is how it will be at the coming of the Son of Man. Two men will be in the field; one will be taken and the other left. **Therefore keep watch, because you do not know on what day your Lord will come.**" (Matt. 24:36-42)

"God's seeming delay in bringing about the consummation of all things is a result of patience in waiting for all who will come to repentance." (NIV Study Bible, pg. 1902)

God gives us many chances to repent. One day while praying for my enemies I asked God why He kept allowing me to be persecuted which was interfering with me accomplishing His Will. He said He is giving them another chance to do what is right. I asked, "How many chances do they get?"

He answered me with this scripture, "Those whom I love I rebuke (reprimand) and discipline. So be earnest, and repent. Here I am! I stand at the door and knock. If anyone hears my voice and opens the door, I will come in and eat with him, and he with me." (Revelations 3:19-20)

God is very patient and persistent in knocking. He will wait for you to open the door to your heart until the very end of time.

No matter what sin you have committed, God has already forgiven it. He is just waiting for your repentance. He is waiting for you to have a change of heart, and He gives us many chances just like He did Pharaoh in the book of Exodus. It is all about our salvation. Everything we do has to benefit God's kingdom.

When I asked God where to tithe He said, "Give to Israel." My Mom said, "I thought we are supposed to give to the poor?" God said, "Give to the poor in spirit." We are supposed to give to those who are spreading God's Word, especially those who are bringing God's Word to people who have never heard it. We can't be saved if we don't know God and you won't know God if you've never heard His Word.

"Maintain justice and do what is right, for the salvation is close at hand and my righteousness will soon be revealed. Blessed is the man who does this, the man who holds it fast, and keeps his hand from doing any evil." (Isaiah 56:1-2)

We must walk as Jesus did. Remember, "God is love. Whoever lives in love lives in God, and God in him." (John 4:8). If you don't know where to begin changing your life, start with how you treat others. Stop thinking you are better than others. We are all equal.

"This is how we know what love is. Jesus Christ laid down his life for us. And we ought to lay down our lives for our brothers." (1John 3:16)

"Do not love the world or anything in the world. If anyone loves the world, the love of the Father is not in him. The world and its desires pass away, but the man who does the Will of God lives forever." (1John 2:15-17)

"Set your minds on things above, not earthly things. Put to death, therefore, whatever belongs to your earthly nature, sexual immorality, impurity, lust, evil desires and greed, which is idolatry. Because of these, the wrath of God is coming. You used to walk in these ways, in the life you once lived. But now you must rid yourselves of all such things as these: anger, rage, malice, slander, and filthy language from your lips. Do not lie to each other, since you have taken off your old self with its practices and have put on the new self, which is being renewed in the knowledge in the image of its Creator. Here there is no Greek or Jew, slave or free, but Christ is, and is in all.

Therefore, as God's chosen people, holy and dearly loved, clothe yourselves with compassion, kindness, humility, gentleness and patience. Bear with each other and forgive whatever grievance you may have against one another. Forgive as the Lord forgave you. And over all these virtues put on love, which binds them all together in perfect unity.

Let the peace of Christ rule in your hearts, and be thankful. Let the Word of Christ dwell in you richly as you teach and admonish one another with all wisdom, and as you sing psalms, hymns and spiritual songs with gratitude in your hearts to God. And whatever you do, whether in word or deed, do it all in the name

of Lord Jesus, giving thanks to God the Father through Him."
(Col. 3:2-17)

"And this is my prayer: that your love may abound more and
more in knowledge and depth of insight, so that you may be able
to discern what is best and may be pure and blameless until the
day of Christ, filled with the fruit of righteousness that comes
through Jesus to the glory and praise of God." (Phil 1:9-11)

**Repent of your sins. Say, "Lord I'm sorry. I'm willing to
change my way of thinking and living, and I'm ready to bring
my whole life under the Lordship of Jesus Christ."**

By faith receive Christ as your Lord and Savior.